THE LEADERSHIP WORKOUT

A PRACTICAL 31-DAY GUIDE TO REVIEW AND REFINE YOUR LEADERSHIP

BRENDA VAN CAMP-ELMES

Copyright © 2019 Brenda van Camp-Elmes

Brenda van Camp has asserted her right to be identified as the
author of this Work in accordance with the Copyrights, Designs and
Patents Act 1988

All rights reserved. No part of this publication may be
reproduced, stored in a retrieval system or transmitted in any form
or by any means, electronic, mechanical, photocopying, recording or
otherwise, without the prior permission of the copyright owner

Published by SPress, Berkeley, California

Printed in the United States of America

ISBN: 9781795434003

For my mother:

*You taught me that where there's
a will there's a way.*

You were right.

Brenda van Camp-Elmes,

February 2019

Table of Contents

Introduction

"It is not wise, or even possible, to divorce private behavior from public leadership.... By its very nature, true leadership carries with it the burden of being an example."

Gordon B. Hinckley

Leadership is not just a set of learnable skills. Rather, effective leadership is an everyday state of mind that guides how we make choices, the ways in which we behave, and the actions we take. However, remaining intentional about leadership is challenging amidst the daily pressures of serial meetings, pending deadlines, and difficult colleagues, to name just a few. Being an intentional leader thus takes deliberate practice.

Moreover, much like physical fitness, leadership capabilities need to be continuously worked on if you want to develop new skills and maintain existing ones. Leadership is not a static skillset that is learned one day and then relied upon and applied for the rest of your career.

The Leadership Workout therefore provides you with a 31-day framework to enable you to purposefully direct and regularly review your leadership through daily reflection and practice, in order to help you refine and further develop your leadership. One facet at a time, one day at a time.

How to use this book: There is no secret logic to how I ordered the reflections. So, you can either read them in order, or pick whichever one you fancy on a given day. However, for this book to have a real impact on your leadership effectiveness, I strongly recommend that you do not just read one reflection a day, but that you actually spend a few minutes each day working through the daily leadership practice which accompanies each reflection. This is important, because only when you connect these reflections to your own experiences as a leader will you gain insights on how you might improve your leadership. Otherwise, it will just remain a lot of talk about abstract concepts and it won't have any impact on your leadership effectiveness going forward. So, I highly recommend you carve out about 10 to 15 minutes at the beginning or end of each day to work through this book one reflection at a time.

Why you should read this book: I'm not going to proclaim that miracles will happen to your leadership effectiveness overnight. Nor do I promise that you will have a major AHA moment after reading each daily reflection. However, I'm fairly certain that by the time you get to day 31 you will most likely have made some significant improvements in your leadership effectiveness, resulting from a combination of many small tweaks, and perhaps one or two big shifts as a result of one or two real AHA moments.

Forewarned is forearmed: At times these reflections may make you feel a little uncomfortable, because they may force you to focus on flaws or weaknesses that you usually try to ignore, because they are incompatible with the conscious image you have of yourself. In those moments I want you to think of this inspiring quote from Trina Paulus: "How does one become a butterfly? You have to want to learn to fly so much that you're willing to give up being a caterpillar." So, it may make you feel a little uncomfortable at times, but don't give in to it, because the fact that you have decided to read this book tells me that you've got what it takes to fly!

Yours sincerely,

Brenda van Camp-Elmes

4

Opposition

*noun, 1. Resistance or dissent,
expressed in action or argument 2. A
group of opponents, especially in sport,
business, or politics.*

A desire for affiliation is one of the 3 key human motivations, alongside power and achievement. However, as a leader we need to be a little wary of our need to surround ourselves with those who agree with us, those who are similar to us, and those who like us.

If we don't, we end up in an echo chamber, and we become isolated from people who have other perspectives, ideas, or access to information that may put things in a whole new light. So, be mindful to not just build relationships with people who you agree with, and who you like, and vice versa.

Instead, proactively seek to develop relationships with competent people who hold opposing ideas, because their opposition will sharpen your thinking. They will reveal perspectives, or possibilities, or threats you had not considered.

Those who oppose you will help you make better considered decisions. Those who agree with you will help you to convince others. You need both.

Keep that in mind when you find yourself in a situation where everyone agrees with you. Step back and find someone who opposes you, because only then might you be saved from stepping into the pitfall, which is right in front of you, but which you did not see, because everyone was agreeing with you.

Today's leadership practice

Identify 1-2 people who currently disagree with you on something, whether it's a project, a solution, or an action.

1. Do you fully grasp why they disagree with you? If not, then make it an action to go see each of them and ask them to explain their different point of view to you. Important note: Do not turn this encounter into a debate. Make it clear that you just want to understand their point of view. Ask questions to ensure you fully grasp their p.o.v. This is also not an opportunity to re-iterate your p.o.v. This is just part of your "discovery" to become fully informed about the different ways to see this project, idea, or issue.

2. Afterwards, write down any new insights that you gained from spending more time engaging with those who disagree with you.

Emotional contagion

noun, 1. the tendency to feel and express emotions similar to and influenced by those of others 2. the phenomenon of one person's negative thoughts or anxiety affecting another's mood.

Emotions are contagious, especially those of a leader. Everyone around you is feeling whether or not you believe in your own vision, in your people's capabilities to achieve it, in the products and services your organization sells, and in the organization as a whole. They just sense it.

You set the tone for your team's emotional climate. You are to be celebrated for its success, or to blame for its failure. Your team's emotional climate is a direct reflection of how you show up each day - your energy and your intention. If you talk incessantly about how busy you are, then your whole team will feel harried and depleted. So, be aware of how you show up. Hold yourself accountable to your leadership philosophy every day. Manage your leadership presence. If you haven't proactively defined either your leadership philosophy or your leadership presence, then make the time to do so. Because if you want to positively impact the culture of your group, then you have to get really intentional about how you show up as a leader each and every day. Because you are contagious!

Today's leadership practice

1. Take a few moments now to reflect on how your emotions are influencing your leadership effectiveness. Think back over the last 2 days at work. Which situations or people triggered your negative emotions and how did you react? The question is not whether your emotions were justified or not. As a leader, you need to consciously manage how you express your emotions. So, take a step back from those moments and assess how your emotions may have helped or hindered the situation or person.

2. Spend 2-3 minutes writing down what you can do differently going forward to handle your emotions more productively with those particular people, or in similar situations.

3. Lastly, for the remainder of today try and pay some extra attention to your emotions. At the end of the day spend a few minutes reflecting on what you've learned about how your emotions may be influencing the people who work with

you, whether those are people on your own team, or your peers, or superiors.

Empowerment

*noun, 1. authority or power given
to someone to do somethings 2. the
process of becoming stronger and more
confident, especially in controlling one's
life and claiming one's rights*

Getting empowerment right as a leader is difficult. Ultimately, your ability to empower your people comes down to you being able to fully trust in your people's clarity about their goals, and in their competence to deliver on them. The trickiest part is that it all starts with you taking the leap of faith that they are competent. Only when you take that leap of faith, will they feel intrinsically motivated to access their full potential and to put in the necessary effort that is needed.

It's somewhat similar to how birds learn to fly. At some point the mother has to stop feeding them and to literally push them out of the nest for them to realize that they can fly and find their own food. As a leader, empowering your people is like pushing them out of the nest, so that they realize that they have what it takes to be successful without your direct guidance.

So, what does this look like on a day-to-day basis. Does it mean you don't have one-to-one's with your people? Does it mean you don't hold people accountable and just let them get on with it? No! It simply means that you should not micro-manage your people. Your role as a leader is to outline and agree clear goals, objectives and standards with them. Once you've done that, then you should rely on their competence to do the detailed planning and to manage the execution to achieve those goals, while you remain available to them as their coach, sounding board, and accountability partner along the way.

Today's leadership practice

Reflect 1-2 minutes on each question and just jot down initial thoughts in response to each question.

1. To what extent do your people have autonomy? What level of decision-making power have you delegated to your direct reports? On what kind of issues do they need to seek your approval or sign off? What are your reasons for putting these controls in place?

2. To what extent do you enable your people to succeed? How much time and effort do you spend coaching them to help develop their competence? (Note that this is not the same as giving them the answers or telling them what to do!!!!!)

3. Having reflected on the above two questions, spend 2-3 minutes now jotting down ideas on which controls you could relinquish and what else you could do to increase your people's empowerment.

4. Actively focus on empowering your people today. Take a few moments at the end of your day to reflect on what you did differently as a result, and to identify any immediate effects or reactions this caused.

Questioning attitude

*noun, a mindset to use continuous
enquiry to develop a deep
understanding of an issue in order to
identify the best course of action.*

Leaders get things done through people. In today's knowledge economy that means you need to engage your people in such a way that they are willing to commit 100% of their brain power to do their job. However, if you are a leader who provides answers, you not only forgo the opportunity to test your decisions, but you also demotivate your people, because your directive approach basically signals to them that you do not value their input. You know best. As a result, your people will commit to just doing enough to get by.

Instead, if you answer their questions with questions, then you signal that you want their involvement, that you believe in their abilities, and that you want them to share the responsibility of finding the best answer. You force them to think, which may make them struggle a bit, but they will like the feeling of finding the answer themselves, which consequently will strengthen their individual learning and their confidence. Moreover, you will benefit from their up-to-date detailed knowledge to help you challenge the answers of yesterday, in order to find the answers to be better tomorrow.

The wise leader thus answers a question with another question to help their people find the answer by themselves. In doing so these leaders develop their people's skills, knowledge and confidence along the way.

Today's leadership practice

Take a few moments to reflect on your own use of questions in your daily leadership

1. Think back to some key decisions you've made or been involved in over the past 6 months.

2. Which of these decisions could have benefitted from more questioning? What questions did you, or other people, fail to ask? Why were these questions not asked?

3. How would you rate your questioning skills?

    - Poor
    - Neither good or bad
    - Good

4. Think of a colleague who is particularly good at questioning. Write down what it is that makes their use of questions so effective.

5. Lastly, commit to having a more questioning attitude today. At the end of the day take a few moments to reflect on how this changed your decisions big or small today.

Radical self-knowledge

*noun, a comprehensive
understanding of one's own
capabilities, character, feelings, or
motivations.*

Radical self-knowledge is fundamental to your leadership journey, both to be able to see what you have to learn or overcome to become a good leader, as well as to know how to collaborate with others to compensate for your weaknesses. Radical self-knowledge is not just about knowing your socially acceptable thoughts, beliefs, and feelings, but also your flaws, primitive negative emotions, and impulses, such as envy, selfishness, desire, and striving for power. As such, radical self-knowledge is hard to embrace, because in everyday life most of us try and ignore our flaws and weaknesses, as they are incompatible with the conscious image we have of ourselves.

Many leadership development programs use a 360° review at the outset of the program to try and create radical self-knowledge. However, most recipients of 360° feedback end up actively denying and rationalizing any feedback they receive on weaknesses or flaws. That is a totally human response, because you simply cannot force self-knowledge upon someone like that.

Instead, to become highly self-aware, you first need to be truly willing to accept that, as Carl Jung said, "I must have a dark side also, if I am to be whole". Only then will you be able to be brutally honest with yourself about the unpleasant attributes in your behavior and personality, and what you have to learn, and how you have to change to become the best leader you can be.

Today's leadership practice

Take a few moments to focus on your self-knowledge with this simple exercise

1. Fold a piece of paper in 2 and use the left column to list your top 10 leadership strengths

2. Now, use the right column to describe an occasion when each of these strengths became a weakness, a flaw, or a blind spot.

3. What new insights about yourself did you gain through this exercise?

DAY 6

Emotional reserves

noun, your well of positive
emotional energy that you have
generated through moments of joy and
connection in your life

Your emotional reserves play a key role in helping you optimize your performance as a leader, because they help you stabilize your temperament, your moods, and your emotions. Your emotional reserves help you to maintain a positive state of mind amidst the daily trials and tribulations of being a leader. It is therefore key that you make sure to regularly refill the well, because once your emotional reserves of positive energy start running low, you become less able to consciously manage your temperament, moods, and emotions and you become more reactionary. When your emotional reserves run low, you start making decisions and taking actions that are instinctive rather than thought-through, and in doing so the quality of your leadership will most likely take a hit.

Unfortunately, many leaders get so usurped by their work that they start sacrificing time with their family, time with their friends, time to pursue their hobbies, and time to just enjoy life. They stop doing exactly those things that would help them refill that important well of positive energy that is critical to support their ability to be the best leader that they can be.

So, self-care is not a nice-to-have. It is a must-have to sustain the emotional energy you need to pursue your journey to the top. If you want to be the best leader you can be, then you need a real commitment to consistent self-care to ensure you have the emotional reserves to fuel your self-control to handle all the daily demands and challenges of leadership!

Today's leadership practice

Let's analyze how you are spending the 168 hours you have each week.

1. Draw a large circle on a large sheet of printer paper. This circle represents all 168 hours of your time & energy each week. Draw two lines to divide the circle into 4 quarters. Each quarter represent 42 hours. So, put 42 at 3 o'clock, 84 at 6 o'clock, 126 at 9 o'clock and finally 168 at 12 o'clock. Now follow these steps to help you re-evaluate how you spend your time and energy.

2. Draw in how much time you sleep, how much time you spend commuting, how much time you spend actually physically at work (in meetings, in

the office, etc.), how much time you spend working at home in the evenings, and how much time you spend working at home in the weekends. To keep them easily identifiable, use a different color for each section and write in each section what they are (sleep, commute, meetings, working at home in the evenings, work on the weekend, etc.)

3. Now start filling in your life outside of work.

    - How much time do you spend on exercise? Differentiate by type of exercise, e.g. yoga, golf, running, etc.

    - How much time do you spend with friends? Differentiate by type of activity, e.g. going out for drinks or dinner, doing an activity together, etc.

    - How much time do you spend relaxing with your family? Differentiate by type of activity, e.g. eating dinner together, just talking together, watching TV, doing an activity together such as going to the movies, playing a sport, going for a walk or to a museum or play, etc.

    Try and map your life out as specifically as possible without losing yourself in the detail, but in such a way that it does give you a meaningful picture of your life

4. Now look at each of these activities. Which of these activities actually give you energy? Put a green plus sign (+) in each section that generates positive emotional energy and put a red minus sign (-/-) in each section that drains you of positive energy. For example, spending time with your partner or going out with friends might take up the least amount of your hours, but they may offer you a lot of positive energy. They make you feel good.

5. Take a moment to reflect on the following questions:

   • How in balance or out of balance is your life map? Do you have enough time invested in activities that generate positive energy, to compensate for the amount of time you spend on activities that actively use up your emotional energy?

   • What activities are time wasters? If they are necessary, such as commuting, how could you transform them to help fill your emotional well? Or do you have the option of avoiding them or replacing them with activities that are more regenerative?

   • What people or activities should you say no to, because they drain your energy?

6. Re-design your life! Redraw your circle by showing how you want to spend your 168 hours per week going forward.

Perfectionism

*noun, a disposition to regard
anything short of perfection as
unacceptable and a sign of personal
worthlessness.*

People often think that perfectionism is a requirement for leadership success, but in doing so they confuse a healthy striving for excellence with perfectionism. Perfectionism is a limiting mindset. Perfectionism is harmful, because it hinders and impairs a leader's ability to take the necessary actions to achieve their goals. Leaders aren't successful because of their perfectionism, but despite their perfectionism. In case you are still not convinced, then let me read out a list of some of the typical harmful behaviors that can result from the having perfectionistic tendencies.

A perfectionist....

- is either too driven, because she can never work hard enough to achieve her unrealistic goals, or she's paralyzed, because she's too afraid to make a mistake.

- is prone to obsess over future results and outcomes, often causing protracted procrastination.
- often pays excessive attention to detail to avoid mistakes, resulting in low productivity.
- is more likely to micro-manage to maintain a sense of control.
- often struggles with delegation due to a lack of trust in other's competence.
- is more likely to avoid risk-taking as she's highly uncomfortable with ambiguity.

So, perfectionism is NOT a must-have leadership trait and if you have any perfectionistic tendencies and aspire to be a great leader, then it would be wise to actively work to learn to control them.

Today's leadership practice

Take a few moments now to reflect on the role of perfectionism in your life, both at home and at work.

1. Have you received any official feedback over the last 2 years which indicates that perfectionistic tendencies may be undermining your performance at work or your relationships outside of work? Have you for example received feedback that you were too involved in the

detail, too controlling, or too concerned about making mistakes?

2. Write down the beliefs that underpin those perfectionistic behaviors. Also, note down what the origins are of these beliefs. Who or what caused you to believe this?

3. Which of the beliefs that fuel your perfectionism is most outdated or unrealistic? What would be a more realistic belief? Write it down and post it in a place where you will be forced to truly see it several times a day

4. Take a moment at the end of today to reflect on how your perfectionism impacted you, your productivity, and your interactions, both at work and at home.

Prioritize

*verb, 1. Determine the order for
dealing with a series of items or tasks
according to their relative
importance 2. Designate or treat
something as more important than
other things*

Great leaders are skilled at the art of triage. They know how to prioritize many demands and how to ensure that they spend their limited time on those issues that are central to their organization's needs. This is why a great leader can remain so focused in their interactions with others. They are able to zone out the competing demands of lesser priorities.

As a leader, your priorities should be clearly defined by your agreed business goals. So, before you allocate time to any relationship, meeting or project, you should ask yourself, "How does this contribute to delivering on my stated business goals?" It's important to truly understand that EVERYTHING ELSE is a distraction until you have handled your priorities. There are no such things as secondary priorities. Many leaders get waylaid by "secondary or tertiary" priorities. But effective leaders prioritize fiercely and focus solely on their key priorities until they are achieved, and only then might these "secondary or tertiary" priorities make it to the top of their list.

A staunch advocate of this approach is Warren Buffett. Mike Flint, who was Buffett's personal airplane pilot for 10 years, shared a story which illustrates Buffett's approach. Flint was talking with Buffett about his career plans when his boss asked the pilot to go through a 3-step exercise. First, Buffett asked Flint to write down his top 25 career goals. So, Flint took some time and wrote them down. Second, Buffett asked Flint to review his list and circle his top 5 goals. Again, Flint took some time, made his way through the list, and eventually decided on his 5 most important goals. Third, when Flint confirmed that he would start working on his top 5 goals right away, Buffett asked him, "And what about the ones you didn't circle?" Flint replied, "Well, the top 5 are my primary focus, but the other 20 come in a close second. They are still important, so I'll work on those intermittently as I see fit. They are not as urgent, but I still plan to give them a dedicated effort." To which Buffett then replied, "No. You've got it wrong, Mike. Everything you didn't circle just became your Avoid-At-All-Costs list. No matter what, these things get no attention from you until you've succeeded with your top 5."

Today's leadership practice

Review and commit to your priorities for the coming week by spending a few minutes working through the following three steps:

1. Write down what you believe your priorities are this coming week.

2. Re-evaluate each of these priorities by asking yourself the following question: "How does this contribute to delivering on my business goals?" Based on this quick evaluation exercise, which projects or issues are a distraction and do not warrant any attention from you until you have taken care of your real priorities?

3. Lastly, ask yourself whether your team is running any projects or initiatives that you should stop, because they are distracting your team from focusing effectively on the real key priorities that will contribute to achieving your team's business goals.

Integrity

*noun, 1. The quality of being
honest and having strong moral
principles. 2. The state of being whole
and undivided*

Integrity is often mentioned as one of the must-have qualities of a great leader, because it is the foundation for the trust others need to have in you to follow you as a leader. But what does it really mean for a leader to show up with integrity every day, in all matters big and small? Integrity is commonly equated with being honest. However, it is much more than that.

Firstly, integrity stems from the Latin word integritas, which means wholeness, and as such the word integrity references a state of congruity, or "integratedness", of everything we feel, say, and do. A leader with high integrity is thus someone who truly lives by their values. They walk their talk.

Secondly, integrity also includes humility, because a person of integrity is more interested in doing the right thing, than being right. Someone who leads with integrity is therefore always open to new ideas and additional information, which may require them to rethink issues. They genuinely put the needs of their organization ahead of their own.

Lastly, integrity also requires courage, the courage to stick by your values and do what is right, even when that comes at a personal cost, or is unpopular or hard.

This all may sound a bit lofty, so here are some examples of basic behaviors to practice integrity on a day to day basis:

- Be truly honest in all your communications. Avoid telling little white lies just for the expediency of the moment.
- Keep your promises. Don't overpromise and then under deliver
- Be open to be influenced. Don't ignore differing points of view, or additional information, even when that complicates the decision-making process.

Though these behaviors may seem simple, integrity is actually a demanding quality to sustain within the context of your everyday reality as a leader. It requires you to be mindful of your values, even under stress, and to always have the self-awareness and self-control to put the needs of your organization ahead of your own ego, and to have the strength of character to do what is right.

Today's leadership practice:

Write the following three bullet points on a note:

- Be honest
- Keep your promises
- Be open

Carry this with you to all your meetings or put it in a place where you see it a lot, so it can act as a physical reminder throughout your day to practice integrity in all matters big and small.

Career planning

noun, an ongoing process through which an individual sets career goals and identifies the means to achieve them.

Many professionals are so busy doing their job that they fail to reflect upon where their career is headed. In management terms, they are so busy with the day-to-day, that they omit to plan for the future until it is too late.

Why do so many smart professionals get caught in this trap? Most people barely plan their lives, let alone their careers. They kind of let them happen more or less. One often heard reason people use to justify this, is that life is unpredictable, and that things will never go according to plan.

It is indeed true that circumstances in your career, as in life, will develop independently, but how you react to your professional circumstances is totally within your control and will determine your future.

When you have a clearly articulated long term career goal, and use this to plot your desired career trajectory, then you are much better equipped to evaluate those circumstances in light of your goal and decide on the best next course of action. You can then be deliberate about what kind of assignments to seek out to develop the skills and experiences you need, and about which relationships you need to build internally and externally. Moreover, you will already have an idea of what you would like your next role to be, so if events overtake you, and you find yourself without a job, you already know what you are looking for next, and you have the contacts to help you find it.

In summary, when you have a career plan, you will be managing your career. Your career won't be managing you.

Today's leadership practice

Take a few minutes now to reflect on your own immediate situation and evaluate your planning for your next career move:

1. What skills or experience are you seeking to gain from your current role? In order to obtain which next role?

2. What measurable impact are you seeking to have in your current role?

3. How will you know that you have acquired the skills and experiences and have had the impact you set out to acquire in this role?

4. How long do you plan to be in this role? What is the shortest amount of time you should do this role without it looking like you are a "restless professional"? What is the longest amount of time you should do this role, i.e. by when would it start to look like you are stagnating?

5. Would getting your desired next role require you to leave your current company?

6. If not, have you expressed this aspiration to your superior(s)? Do you have an explicit agreed plan in place, including agreed performance milestones, to eventually be promoted to that role?

7. If you have to leave your current employer for your next role, then which potential employers could provide you with that next role? Do you have relationships with people who currently work at these companies? Do you have relationships with headhunters who recruit for such roles at these companies?

Productive conflict

*noun, an open exchange of
conflicting or differing ideas in which
parties feel equally heard, respected,
and unafraid to voice dissenting
opinions for the purpose of reaching a
mutually comfortable resolution.*

Conflict is an undeniable part of working in
an organization. Wishing for a conflict-free
work environment is unrealistic and
pretending to have such an environment is
undesirable. In fact, the philosophy that underpins
some of today's most successful companies is the
notion that you must combine the energy, ideas, and
knowledge of diverse perspectives to find answers
to complex problems. Such teams, composed of
high-performing individuals, are naturally subject to
contradictory tensions, like cooperation and rivalry,
trust and vigilance. These tensions should not be
managed away, because they are productive and can
help teams perform better. As a leader you must
thus develop the skills to engage with conflict in a

productive way in order to generate the best possible decisions and outcomes. Here are 3 key strategies to help you do so:

Make it safe for people to share their divergent opinions: Most people are concerned about stating their opinion for fear of being proven wrong. So, instead of asking people to state their personal opinion or POV, start by inviting everyone to help you brainstorm or list different approaches, points of views, and solutions. This provides a safe way for people to contribute, because they are just helping you take stock of all the possible angles.

Facts over feelings: If you want constructive conflict, then you need to set a clear expectation that all opinions must be supported by data and facts. Personal opinions, feelings, hunches, and emotions stand in the way of rational objectivity and conflict resolution. Compel your team members to prepare their fact-based arguments beforehand, and you'll have a much more productive conversation

Task people with proving their own opinions wrong: We accept in the abstract that people can be wrong, but when we think about ourselves, we lack the ability to understand that we may be wrong. A great way of opening people up to a more expansive way of thinking is to task them with proving their own solution wrong, and to then ask them to form counter arguments to prove those wrong again. This will teach your team members to be more resilient and open minded.

Today's leadership practice

Getting skilled at using conflict as a productive tool in a safe way takes time & effort. To get started, take a few minutes now to reflect on the following questions

1. Explore your own relationship with conflict: Are you comfortable with using conflict productively to discuss ideas and solutions, or do you avoid it at all costs? Do you have an example of another leader who is skilled at it? What does he or she do that works?

2. Explore your team's relationship with conflict: Does everyone on your team feel comfortable challenging you as well as each other? If not, then review some of the reasons that commonly make people avoid conflict. Which of the following reasons may be causing your people to avoid productive conflict?

   • They avoid making a clear statement about their position for fear of alienating some of their affiliations
   • They rather play it safe for fear of being proven wrong
   • They don't want to rock the boat by disagreeing for fear of being perceived as a troublemaker
   • They don't feel it's worth the trouble, and they believe others will speak-up, so they don't have to.

- They are afraid to offend their boss or colleague

3. Experiment: Commit this week to using the above-mentioned strategies in some of the meetings you chair. Start with leading by example by asking others to help prove your idea, opinion, or solution wrong, and make a point of backing up your own ideas, opinions or decisions with data and facts. Nudge others in the new direction by gently introducing these new practices. At the end of each day, write down any lessons learned from your experiments.

Control

noun, the power to influence or direct people's behavior or the course of events.

Controlling behavior is one of the most common and wide-spread dysfunctions of leaders, often born out of a leader's own deep-seated sense of insecurity, and need for validation and approval. Typical examples of controlling behaviors are the following:

- Micro-managing
- Delegating tasks rather than responsibility
- Obsessing about the smallest errors
- Limiting the autonomy of underlings and associates
- Keeping close tabs on those around them through excessive meetings and reporting

Such controlling behavior may make a leader feel more directly in control of the deliverables for which they are responsible. However, it has a hugely negative impact on people's intrinsic motivation, because it negates their need for autonomy and responsibility, which are two key drivers of intrinsic motivation. As a result, employees will take less ownership of their work, be less creative, less productive, and less effective in problem solving, requiring a leader to manage the work more closely.

Interestingly, this may then cause a leader to think she or he was right to maintain control, because her team clearly wasn't yet up to the task. However, in truth, the leader is the problem as her need for control destroyed the team's intrinsic motivation, and with that their willingness to use discretionary effort and their full potential to deliver the task as best they could.

Today's leadership practice

Spend a few minutes now to ponder the following 4 questions:

1. Which of your management processes and policies are limiting your team's levels of self-determination and autonomy?

2. Think of some negative incidences that have been caused by your need for control.

3. How would better regulating your need for control improve your leadership effectiveness?

4. What proactive actions can you undertake to improve your self-management of your need for control?

Character

*noun, the complex of mental and
ethical traits marking and often
individualizing a person, group, or
nation*

C haracter is fundamental to effective leadership, because good character builds trust, and without trust, people will not follow you, and without followers, obviously, one cannot lead. However, in this age of individuality we rarely talk about what defines good character.

John Maxwell, the leadership development expert, identified four key building blocks to develop strong character:

Self-discipline & moral courage: To do what is right, even if you don't feel like it – i.e. to practice the self-control to balance your own desires with the needs of others, and the courage also to face the fears, risks, and dangers of standing up for what is right.

Core values: A clear sense of the values that guide your behavior every day.

A sense of identity: Truly knowing yourself and your beliefs. The second stanza of Rudyard Kipling's poem "If" perfectly captures this concept, "If you can trust yourself when all men doubt you, but make allowance for their doubting too."

Integrity: The practice of aligning your actions, feelings, and thoughts with your values.

The tricky part is that you cannot just "put those building blocks in place" and be done with it. Our character is the result of a series of consistent choices over a length of time. Our character is formed every time we face a defining moment that challenges us to sort through our core values and principles. If we are willing to use our self-discipline and self-control to try and do the right thing, each and every time, during those defining moments, then over time these decisions will shape our personal and professional identities. So, character is not just talk. It is not just a matter of knowing who you are and what your values are. Your character, which is the balance of your values, virtues and vices, expresses itself through your actions, and that is the foundation of your leadership.

Today's leadership practice

Spend a few minutes now to ponder the following 5 questions:

1. What are your non-negotiables in life and work? What won't you accept from others and from yourself? What are your big-time deal breakers?

2. Think of an occasion or decision at work that made you feel very uncomfortable. Which value(s) did it challenge?

3. After pondering the above two questions, can you write down the 5 key principles that are the guard rails for how you live and lead every day?

4. Do you express these principles and values regularly, so that people know what to expect from you?

5. After reflecting on these questions, what small change can you commit to for the next week, to ensure your actions are better aligned with your values and principles?

Bad leadership

*Bad: adjective, 1. of poor quality
or a low standard 2. not such as to be
hoped for or desired; unpleasant or
unwelcome.*

*Leadership: noun, the action of
leading a group of people or an
organization*

Most of us think of ourselves as pursuing 'good leadership'. In reality, however, we do not always exercise our power, use our authority, or exert our influence in ways that are good. It is the very nature of our human condition, our emotionality, ambition and desires, that provides a constant background challenge for any leader's 'goodness'. Philosophers, such as Aristotle, Hobbes, Rousseau, and Locke, have all noted that, unless there are clear restraints in place, power is certain to be abused in small or big ways. It's this understanding that has for example also guided the writers of the American Constitution to include the various checks and balances to guard against bad leadership.

Most people in leadership roles vacillate on an almost daily basis between being both good and bad leaders. Their overall intention is to be a good leader, but as the pressure cooker of leadership heats up, their dark side bubbles to the surface, triggering, for example, paranoid, controlling, rigid, intemperate, or arrogant behavior. Their behavior may not be as egregious as that of former Enron leaders Kenneth Lay and Jeffrey Skilling, but these behaviors nevertheless undermine their leadership effectiveness.

However, most leaders do not even realize they are at times being a bad leader. Why not? Because the moment we act in a way that is incongruous with our intentions to be a good leader, our brain recognizes the cognitive dissonance and jumps into action to find a justification. We self-justify our actions constantly to explain them away. We play favorites between our direct reports, but claim our choice was based on merit. We micro-manage, but say we stay really close to the action to help get the work done. We have an angry outburst and we say it was necessary to imbue a real sense of urgency. Etcetera.

Moreover, though few leaders will admit that they regularly fall foul to bad leadership behavior, it does not go unnoticed by those who work for them. In fact, studies suggest that 1 in 4 leaders are seen as bad or destructive leaders. This means that more of us may be seen as bad leaders than we think. It is therefore important for any leader to be honest with themselves and to acknowledge how they sometimes fall short of being a good leader and to be proactive about developing strategies to get ahead of these bad leadership tendencies. As Abraham Lincoln so aptly said: "All human beings have their weaknesses, but not all of us realize them, come to grips with them, or offset their negative impact. As a group whose primary endeavor is interacting with other people, leaders must accomplish the paradoxical task of managing their darker sides."

Today's leadership practice

Spend a few minutes now to ponder the following 4 questions:

1. What are the 2 bad behavioral tendencies that you most want to change or eliminate?

2. What drives you to behave in those ways?

3. What are the potential negative consequences for your leadership effectiveness?

4. What could you do to better control those bad behavioral tendencies going forward?

Curiosity

noun, the desire to learn or know
more about something or someone

Curiosity is key to effective leadership, because it leads to well-informed decisions and drives progress. However, in reality, few business people actively practice curiosity, due to a variety of reasons that conspire to undermine it.

Firstly, many of us tend to be too pushed for time to be inquisitive, whether in a meeting, on the phone or via email. We don't have the time to give everything our full attention. We sign off on a decision when a proposed course of action sounds logical, rather than asking questions to explore alternative routes. On top of that, many of us also self-censor our questioning, because we either fear that asking questions is an admission of ignorance, or because we think questioning may be perceived as "being difficult", or as second-guessing someone's expertise or judgment.

Secondly, as we advance in our careers, we have a considerable amount of accumulated knowledge and experience, which may cause us to think we already know everything. This is sometimes referred to as the "over-confidence effect", and this can lead people to make disastrous decisions based on outdated information.

Lastly, many of us are also generally too busy to read much, or to attend a conference for the sheer purpose of learning rather than being a speaker.

As a leader you need to take proactive action to counter each of these tendencies, because your curiosity is critical to the effectiveness of your leadership.

Here are three key steps to help you reignite the power of curiosity in your everyday leadership:

Make a conscious effort to lead through questions rather than answers. To do so, you need to cultivate the habit of always taking a few minutes before each meeting to ask yourself what questions you would like to have answered during the meeting.

Learn how to approach issues with a truly open mind and to not jump to conclusions. You need to be willing to consider an issue from multiple angles as well as to have your own ideas and arguments proven wrong.

Make time to read, because as president Truman so aptly said, "Not all readers become leaders. But all leaders must be readers." If you are not already doing this, start small by just blocking out 20 minutes 3 times per week to read 3 key business publications, whether online or offline. Your aim is to keep up with what is happening in your industry, your area of functional expertise and the wider world of business.

Today's leadership practice

Re-ignite your curiosity by focusing on these 2 simple actions today

1. Tell your team and peers that you are on the hunt for interesting articles about the future of your industry or area of expertise. Ask them to forward you links to such articles whenever they come across them.

2. Make it your focus today to ask many simple questions to deepen the conversation with others about the issues at hand. Don't overthink it. Ask things such as:

    *   Why do you think that is the case?

    *   What impact would that have on our employees, customers or vendors?

    *   How can we explore that further?

    *   Who can do that for us?

    *   What is the reason for that?

    *   How else could we look at this? What assumptions are you making?

Storytelling

noun, the activity of telling or writing stories

The time of management by decree is well and truly over. To engage their people, today's leaders have to communicate not just what, but also why. To move people to action it isn't enough anymore to just provide a logical argument, because people don't tend to be inspired by reason alone. PowerPoint decks, however cogent the argument, fail to make people care. Today's leaders need to arouse their people's emotions, enthusiasm and energy. And that is why storytelling has become a key skill in the communications toolkit of the effective leader.

Some of you may still doubt whether stories are really appropriate in business. They are, when used correctly. Good business arguments should still be developed through the analysis of hard facts and logic. However, stories help people associate the argument with real life. It helps them see it. That is why management books always encourage leaders to use "vivid language" to communicate their key ideas and concerns to bring it to life, so people can almost see it. For example, Steve Denning used the simple story below to help galvanize his staff at the World Bank to support his vision of building a knowledge management platform that would enable them to put the World Banks vast know-how at the fingertips of those who most needed it. His story went like this: "In June of 1995, a health worker in a tiny town in Zambia went to the website of the Centers for Disease Control (CDC) and got the answer to a question about the treatment for malaria. Remember that this was in Zambia, one of the poorest countries in the world, and it happened in a tiny place, 600 kilometers from the capital city. But the most striking thing about this picture, at least for us, is that the World Bank isn't in it. Despite our know-how on all kinds of poverty-related issues, that knowledge isn't available to the millions of people who could use it. Imagine if it were. Think what an organization we could become." Initially this approach may feel a bit contrived and awkward, like writing with your opposite hand. But keep trying because this is not a fad. People connect to stories.

Today's leadership practice

Take a few minutes now to give this a try by working through this exercise to help you craft a short story vignette which quickly conveys what you stand for as a leader. We refer to this as a "Who I Am" story vignette, and it is an incredibly powerful leadership tool.

1. Compose a story vignette about yourself that would reveal an experience that led to a certain belief or conviction that is manifest and core to your leadership approach. Choose one of the following three approaches, or, if you feel inspired, then try to write a separate story vignette for each, as they are all three very helpful in conveying to your team, your boss, and your peers what you stand for.

    Story #1: My Value – What is a value that you are living? What early experience in your life taught you about that important value?

    Story #2: Moment of Pride – When did you achieve something important in your life? Why was that moment important to you?

    Story #3: Moment of Learning – When did you take a risk and failed at something? What valuable lessons did you learn from it?

2. Use your vignettes: Look for opportunities this week to share your story vignette(s) to illustrate what you stand for as a leader or to convey what you value.

Charisma

*noun, 1. a personal magic of
leadership arousing special popular
loyalty or enthusiasm for a public
figure 2. a special magnetic charm or
appeal*

Many people think charisma is this magical skill that only a few people possess. It isn't. It is just interpersonal influence practiced at the highest level. And it is learnable. And the actual skills underlying it are easy and within the grasp of anyone. It just takes doing something very different from what most of us do: In a world where everyone is focused on themselves 95% of the time, it means making a deliberate effort to 100% focus on connecting and relating to others when in the presence of others.

For example, people often mention former President Bill Clinton's ability to make anyone feel that they truly matter to him. The skill that underlies Bill Clinton's impact on others is his "focused attention", which means that he makes solid eye contact and truly listens to what a person has to say. That sounds so simple, but it is something that very few of us practice.

We live in a time where no one pays attention to anyone for more than a few seconds. We're always multi-tasking. We listen to someone and at the same time we're in the back of our mind also thinking about our response, or about how the others in the room are reacting, or what we need to do later, or that we actually feel like having a coffee or a glass of water. Similarly, we have gotten used to checking our phone whenever it rings or beeps, just to quickly see who we need to call or message or email back later. It is therefore truly rare when someone ignores anything or anyone else and just pays 100% attention to you and what you have to say.

So, though focused attention is a skill anyone can master to boost their charisma, it requires a lot of self-control to resist distractions and it also requires a real commitment to being truly other-focused.

Today's leadership practice

Commit to practicing so-called third level listening this week, because this is key to strengthening your focused attention. Here are three key pointers to help you on your way:

1. Don't just listen to the words the other person is uttering. Instead, listen with all your senses and intuition in order to also pick up on the speaker's feelings, energy level and what isn't being said.

2. Do not listen as a judge or critic, but more as a neutral 'receiver'.

3. Use your self-awareness to stay non-defensive, because otherwise it is impossible to stay focused on another person.

Differences

noun, a point or way in which
people or things are not the same.

We are drawn to people who are similar, because we understand them. We can predict their behavior. We enjoy the fact that they understand us. They make us feel stronger and affirmed.

People who are different from us make us uncomfortable. They make us wonder whether we are wrong. They act in ways we don't understand. They make us feel weaker.

However, it is exactly in those differences that our combined strength lies, not in the comfort of our overlapping beliefs, values, and ideas. This may sound like a platitude, but many of us regularly choose comfort over challenge

As leaders in business, we need to remind ourselves of this whenever we create and work with teams. We prefer to work with people who are similar because you can go faster, but are you sure your outcome is as good as it could be? We want things to go easy and smooth, but is that really the path to the best outcome?

Different is difficult and unsettling ... Because it challenges us to let go of the certainty and safety of our beliefs, and to consider that our perspective may not be the only answer. It challenges us to embrace the ambiguity of dealing with multiple possible ways, perspectives, or answers.

Different is slower .... Because it requires us to suspend judgment and decisions until we have considered the different approaches and possibilities.

Different is fractious .... Because it requires us to highlight our differences, rather than smooth them over. It requires us to proactively disagree.

Yet different is better .... Because through this difficult, unsettling, slow and fractious process we gather new perspectives, ideas, possible answers and ways of doing things, creating a treasure trove from which a better answer, idea, or approach will likely arise.

As leaders we need to embrace the fact that collaboration should not be smooth sailing. We need to accept that harmony is not the ideal. So, instead of seeking to create teams in which all differences have been blunted into a smooth harmonious whole, we need to build teams which truly foster and leverage the diversity of thinking generated by people from different generations, genders, orientations, cultures, and personalities.

Today's leadership practice

Commit to finding the value in differences this week.

1. Make it a point this week to seek out and celebrate different perspectives on all kinds of issues.

2. Invite someone from another department to attend a meeting on a key issue your team is trying to deal with and ask them to share their viewpoints on the issue from their different perspective.

3. Challenge your own thinking this week. Make it a routine this week to try and view things through other people's eyes. How would you see this issue if you were the CEO? Or if you were running your peer's department? How would you view this if you were a millennial? Etcetera.

4. Take a few moments at the end of each day to reflect on how this practice impacted you and your team in your decisions, actions or ideas.

Halo effect

*noun, the human tendency to
assume that a person's superior status
means that they must have superior
skills, traits and knowledge.*

Though not all leaders realize this, leadership does not mean that you personally need to be the originator or creator of all the main solutions or ideas. As per Kouzes and Posner in their book The Leadership Challenge, "The leader's primary contribution is in recognizing and supporting good ideas". The key word here is "recognizing". They suggest a leadership style that searches for solutions from others.

However, many leaders, and maybe even some of you, may now think, "But my employees never bring me any useful ideas." This is, however, often a result of a leader's halo effect, whereby employees do not speak up, with ideas or counter arguments, because they respect the leader and they believe he or she probably knows better and has better information. Employees will often self-silence to avoid seeming disagreeable and disrespectful to the boss, even if they have information that points in another direction or that directly disputes the leader's solution. This is why much important information or good ideas frequently fail to reach a leader, thereby ultimately undermining his or her leadership effectiveness.

Today's leadership practice

Take the following two actions this week to proactively mitigate the effect of your leader's halo:

1. Silence your desire to show off your expertise and experience, and instead focus first on what your team's views are. Use questioning to truly understand their views, ideas, or concerns. Only add your own opinion, if need be, at the end. Remind yourself of this by writing SPEAK LAST in the top right-hand corner of the pages of your notebook. (Go ahead. Do it now. Write it in the top right-hand corner of the next 30 pages or so.)

2. Make it psychologically safe for your people to oppose your ideas and decisions, or to raise concerns about them. Communicate explicitly to your team that you don't just want them to be yes-sayers. For example, state this explicitly at the beginning of every meeting that you chair. Consider also whether you've implemented policies or have any bad habits that "punish" people for disagreeing with you. If so, take steps to resolve this.

Outsight

noun, vision or perception of external things; the capacity to see or observe; (the ability to take) an overview.

A leader's outsight is their up-to-date knowledge of social, technological, economic, environmental, and political trends and events, that could affect their vendors, employees, competitors or customers and thereby their business. Such outsight is a key leadership competency, because it is foundational for a leader's ability to develop the strategic foresight that is required to outline the preferred future. Note though that developing your outsight is not just a case of being a voracious reader and networker. Just exposing yourself to lots of information sources doesn't automatically help you find new answers to existing complex issues or provide you with strategic foresight. Information only becomes outsight when you analyze and evaluate the information to form your own judgment about how it will affect your business and what the resulting opportunities or challenges are. So, the formula for outsight is:

Information input + Thinking = Outsight

I appreciate that some of you may start to feel that this is just going to require too much of your time. Time you don't have. But bear with me. What we're suggesting is just a shift in mindset, whereby you train yourself to make it a habit to ask questions while consuming information in order to explore its meaning and effect. Questions such as:

- What is the main idea or theory underpinning this?
- If this is true, what is likely to happen as a result?
- If this is true, then what else is true?
- What happens when we act on that belief or idea?
- How might others react to this?

You'll be surprised how a lot of information, which you are already consuming, will become much more meaningful when you approach it in this way.

Today's leadership practice

Take a moment now to actually apply this. Select an article you have earmarked in a magazine that is lying on your desk, or an article in an e-newsletter which you have flagged in your email inbox. While reading it, ask yourself the following meaning-making questions:

- What is the main idea or theory underpinning this?
- If this is true, what is likely to happen as a result?
- If this is true, then what else is true?
- What happens when we act on that belief or idea?
- How might others react or respond to this?

Persuasion

*noun, the act of causing people to
do or believe something: the act or
activity of persuading people*

Leaders spend a lot of time convincing others to change their point of view, and most leaders figure that words, well-chosen and expertly delivered, will help them to do that. The reality is that verbal persuasion often comes across as an attack. In fact, whenever you as a leader use forceful and overt verbal persuasion to try and convince others to see things your way, they are probably not even listening to what you say. Instead, they are looking for every error in your logic and every mistake in your facts, all the while constructing counterarguments. They don't just believe you're wrong, they need you to be wrong.

So, how else are you as a leader supposed to help them see things your way? The operative word here is SEE. People are more likely to change their mind when you help them to see things for themselves – i.e. personal experience is the best persuader. For example, instead of trying to persuade your boss or your team by surprising them with a hard-hitting presentation of your charts and tables at the next meeting, send them the underlying data, or share the voice of the customer straight from the horse's mouth, well in advance of your meeting. Accompany this by some well-worded questions which guide their eyes to spot the things you want them to SEE and analyze for themselves.

Another way of helping others SEE things is to tell a story, which allows them to truly picture the issue in a real-world scenario. When told well, a detailed story of an event can help listeners to drop their doubts as to the validity of your proposed action. You want your story to create a vicarious experience for your audience. So, you may require some props, such as photos, video or direct quotes to really bring your story to life. For example, we know a leader who was the global head of marketing for a large international art company. She was in the middle of a company-wide skirmish about who controlled the communication to their top clients. Most departments wanted to hear nothing of it. They wanted to be able to market to any client whenever they saw fit.

However, she knew they were hurting their client relationships through that approach, but her suggestions fell on deaf ears and even got her into some trouble, until she told them the story of a client, who was one of their top 500 clients. This client had been buying art across multiple categories and across varying price levels, ranging from a pair of fabulous 17th century English silver candle sticks to a gorgeous early Picasso and a number of rare and beautifully carved Japanese netsukes. As a result of the lack of control over who got to market to this client, he had received 401 pieces of marketing collateral in the mail in the last year. She asked her team to use their marketing archive to put together a complete collection of each of the 401 pieces he had been send. They needed 7 boxes to carry them into the meeting. Let's just say that this helped her peers and superiors see why she was so passionate about the need to put some controls in place.

So, next time when you are trying to dislodge old ways of thinking or to convince others of the validity of your approach, don't give in to your inclination to use verbal gymnastics and overwhelm them with your charts and tables. Instead, ask yourself how you can help them SEE it for themselves, whether that is by telling them a story, or by giving them the clues, so they can do their own detective work and come to the same conclusion.

Today's leadership practice

Select an issue on which you are trying to influence one or more people to change their mind. Take a few minutes now to work through the following two questions to help you develop a way to make them see it your way without using verbal persuasion.

1. How can you help your colleagues EXPERIENCE the issue? Start by sketching out a short story vignette that paints the picture

in a real-world scenario. Try describing it as a cause and effect story.

2. What raw data points or facts could you compile and share? What objective guidance could you add to direct their attention to SEE what you are seeing?

Fail point

*noun, event or circumstance which
could negatively impact the outcome of
a planned endeavor*

A critical step to de-risking your key business decisions as a leader, is to spend ample time predicting all that could negatively impact the desired outcome and be ready with a response. Most teams therefore spend a lot of time considering and preparing responses for all kinds of external factors, such as competitive moves, or potentially negative macro-economic and political events. However, the biggest fail points in business decisions, though often overlooked, come from within the organization:

First of all, we should never overlook our **planning bias**, which frequently makes us too optimistic about how little time and resources we will need, or how supportive our internal and external partners will be.

In addition, we should also **make sure that everyone involved has both the capacity and the capabilities** to execute as required. Capacity and capability are two very different things. A team or team member may have the capacity but not the required skills or expertise, or they may have the capabilities but not the bandwidth to take on the required task(s).

And last, even when everyone involved has the capabilities and capacity to execute, you also need to **make sure that everyone is truly committed to do what it takes.**

Planning bias and these 3 Critical C's, capabilities, capacity and commitment, are the 4 major potential fail points of most important business decisions and these 4 potential fail points should be part of your routine check list to de-risk key decisions.

Today's leadership practice

Take a moment now to actually apply this to an endeavor you are about to give the go-ahead on. Use the questions below to evaluate each of the internal fail points in detail and to decide how to best handle them.

1. What happens if the planned timelines are too optimistic? What events or circumstances could interfere with your planned timelines? What can you do to avoid those circumstances from

interfering with your timelines? What, if anything, can you do if that happens?

2. What happens if you underestimated your resource requirements? What events or circumstances could cause you to need more resources than planned? What, if anything can you do to avoid this or to handle this if it happens?

3. Do all the stakeholders have the capacity to fulfill their task? What events or circumstances could interfere with your stakeholders' capacity to fulfill their tasks? What, if anything can you do to avoid this or to handle this if it happens?

4. Do all the stakeholders have the required capabilities to successfully fulfill their tasks? What events or circumstances could negatively impact your stakeholders' capabilities to fulfill their tasks? What can you do to avoid those events or circumstances or what would you do if that happens?

5. Are all the stakeholders fully committed to support the endeavor? What could weaken their commitment? What can you do to ensure they remain committed throughout?

Lead indicator

noun, an indicator that predicts
future events and tends to change
ahead of that event

S trategic goal setting is a key part of any leader's role. However, too often leaders find out too late in the game that they will not achieve their strategic goal(s) as planned, because they failed to determine how they would be able to measure whether their actions actually resulted in progress towards their goal(s). For example, let's imagine we work for an online apparel business, and that our strategic goal is to improve the customer experience, as measured by the Net Promotor Score (NPS), by improving it from a score of 40 to a score of 52. The NPS metric is what we call a lag metric. This means that it is an outcome and we cannot influence the lag metric, because it is an after-the-event measurement. To measure how well we are progressing towards our goal, we instead need to look for lead indicators, which are in-process measures, and which are predictive of our ability to achieve our goal.

Using our earlier example, let's imagine that research suggested that on time delivery is a key driver of customer satisfaction. We might then consider using *% of orders delivered on time* as a key lead indicator. In addition, we might find that having 3 or more customer reviews for each product is also a key driver of customer satisfaction. Another lead indicator might therefore be *% of sku's with 3 or more customer reviews*. So, in order to achieve a certain goal, your people shouldn't focus on the lag measure of the goal itself, but on the lead measures that drive the goal.

In case of our example, this thus means that they shouldn't focus on the NPS score, but should focus instead on the most important actions that will drive an increase in the *% of orders that is delivered on time,* as well as any actions that increase the *% of SKU's that have more than 3 customer reviews*, because by doing so they will eventually achieve their goal.

Taken together, immediately after establishing your strategic goal(s), make sure you and your team take the time to determine what the key performance drivers are to help them achieve the goal(s), and what the lead indicators are to keep track of their progress on moving those drivers.

Today's leadership practice

Select one of the strategic initiatives you and your people are currently pursuing. Take a moment to reflect on the following questions regarding said initiative:

1. What is the lag metric for your strategic goal?

2. What are the key performance drivers that your people need to influence in order to achieve that strategic goal?

3. What are the lead metrics to measure how your people are moving those performance drivers in order to progress towards the goal?

Appreciative inquiry

Appreciative: adjective, valued; recognizing the best in people or the world around us; affirming past and present strengths, successes, and potentials; perceiving those things that give life (health, vitality, excellence) to living systems

Inquiry: noun, a seeking or request for truth, information, or knowledge.

Deficit-based problem solving is the widely accepted and practiced way to strategic thinking and management. We use it to assess how to best overcome the obstacles on our path to realizing our company's future vision, or when we review progress against the agreed milestones and KPIs by asking questions such as "What can we do about problem xyz? When does problem xyz occur? Why does problem xyz occur? How can we solve the root causes of problem xyz?"

However, extensive research by behavioral psychologists has proven that such a constant focus on what needs to be fixed in your organization actually makes us less able to perform at our best, because it narrows our attention and limits our depth of perception and undermines our ability to think creatively. Instead, leaders should consider using an approach called "Appreciative Inquiry" to resolve issues and create organizational change. Appreciative Inquiry doesn't ignore problems, it just chooses to approach them differently by focusing on the following three principles:

1. **What we focus on becomes our reality** – If we focus on problems, we can find problems everywhere. If taken too far this can create a sense that it is all unsurmountable. If we instead focus on what has been possible when we were at our best, you all of a sudden create tremendous positive energy.

2. **The act of asking questions causes us to develop new perspectives**, which in turn causes us to start changing our behavior, because we can now no longer operate automatically in the ways we did before we started asking questions about things.

3. **People commit to what they create** and can envision themselves.

So, instead of focusing on what needs to be fixed in order to achieve the desired change, a leader or organization that practices appreciative leadership focuses on asking questions about how the business had operated when it was very successful - i.e. when the problem(s) didn't occur - and uses that as a basis to build its plan for the future. To do so the leader would ask questions such as, "What were the conditions when the problem didn't occur, and the team/organization was performing at its best? How did people operate when the problem didn't occur, and the team/organization was performing at its best?"

Focusing on past moments of success is also critical in helping to create buy-in for change because it communicates that leadership recognizes and greatly values the abilities of the existing organization. This approach thus avoids the downside of the traditional problem-solving approach to change, which usually causes many people to feel criticized, because the focus is all about finding fault with what has been done in the past.

Lastly, focusing the organization on positive moments in its past also plays a key role in re-energizing the workforce by helping people to regain their confidence in their abilities to be successful, which in turn reignites their passion and commitment to put in their best efforts to help the business to reclaim its success.

In summary, Appreciative Inquiry is a powerful leadership tool to help teams and organizations build their capacity for change, but it requires a fundamental shift in thinking.

Today's leadership practice

Learning to effectively use Appreciative Inquiry takes commitment and some training, but you can start applying the basics today by making a shift in how you solve for change. To help get you started take a few moments now to ponder the following questions:

1. Think of a strategic goal your team or organization is pursuing. Instead of asking, "What is standing in our way of achieving this goal or change?" ask "What did we do when we were performing at our best? How could we leverage or build on those strengths to create bold change in the direction of our desired future?"

2. Think of a problem or issue your team or organization is facing. Instead of asking "What is the root cause of this issue?" ask, "What were the conditions when we did not have this issue? What would we have to do to recreate those conditions? How did we operate when we did not have this issue? How can we ensure we always operate like that?"

Budget versus forecast

*Budget: noun, an estimate of
income and expenditure for a set
period of time*

*Forecast: noun, a prediction or
estimate of future events, especially
coming weather or a financial trend*

The terms budgeting and forecasting are frequently used interchangeably. However, they are two different processes with different purposes. The key difference between a budget and a forecast is that the budget is a plan for where a business wants to go, while the forecast is an estimate of what the company will actually achieve if it keeps performing as it does. So, when you compare the forecast to the budget, it shows you where you end up if you do nothing to course correct. The forecast thus shows you to what extent you will end up off-target, if you continue as is.

Now, the danger lies in the fact that leaders at times start (mis-)using the forecast as a quick re-budget to reconfirm targets and to manage expectations internally and externally. When misinterpreted like this, organizations can end up budgeting 13 to 15 times a year and will surely end up widely off-target compared to the original budget.

Instead, the correct approach is to use the forecast as an early-warning system to inform your dynamic decision-making about which remedial steps to take in order to bring the actual results back in line with the budget! So, the forecast is a tool to help you stay on track to meet your budget, but the forecast NEVER BECOMES the budget!

Today's leadership practice

Take a moment now to compare the latest forecast for your area of the business against its original budget. Carefully review the deviations between the forecast and the budget and explore whether you and your team have made the necessary tactical adjustments as reality unfolds along the way, to ensure you will still meet your goal. In doing so, don't get too distracted by the %s. For example, a small 5% variance in a large revenue or expense line can be more positive or negative than a large 20% deviation in a small budget line. Moreover, sometimes the numbers may look in line with the budget, but the underlying drivers may vary from your original assumptions. For example, it may look like your overall revenues are tracking well against budget, but when you look closer it does show that you are selling more than expected of one product line and less than expected of another product line.

This may look fine, but what if their gross margins aren't the same? Then that could have a major impact on profitability....

Brainpower

*noun, intellectual capacity; mental
ability*

Your brain is your most important tool to help you perform as a leader. It's therefore in your best interest to deeply understand how it operates on a physical level, so that you know how to optimize its performance.

The first thing to know is that your brain is the organ that uses the most of your energy. It uses about 25% of all the energy your body produces by breaking down the sugar from the food you eat. This means that *when* you eat and *what* you eat has a real impact on your cognitive function. Though we all know this, few of us take it seriously. For example, many professionals skip breakfast as they are in a rush to get to the office on time. Yet, what's the use of that if you arrive at the office with barely any energy in your tank to fuel your brain?

Another thing to know about your brain is that it consists for 75% of water, so it should come as no surprise that dehydration has a dramatic effect on your brain function. Simply said, your brain sans water is like a cell phone without charge. So, you need to drink up! For optimum performance, it is recommended to divide your body weight by 2 as a guide to how many ounces of water you should drink each day. Also, it is recommended to drink a glass of water as soon as you wake up, because you will have lost a lot of water during sleep. You literally have to "water your brain", if you want to wake up and feel sharp. And remember, coffee dehydrates, so that 16 oz. Starbucks does NOT count towards hydrating your brain

The third thing to know about your brain is that it requires 7-8 hours of sleep each day to complete a daily maintenance cycle to ensure the optimal performance of your cognitive function. Many people still see sleep as a waste of time, but the brain is far from doing nothing when you sleep. One of the central functions of sleep is that it helps you consolidate long term memories, because it uses your sleeping hours to strengthen neural connections and to prune unwanted ones. That is why sleep helps you remember things you learned during the day. Secondly, during your sleeping hours your brain also increases the speed at which it clears out toxins. A lot of this gunk is B-amyloid protein, which is the precursor of the plaques in Alzheimer's disease. So, sleep is critical for the optimal performance of your cognitive function in the short AND long term.

I am of course well aware that many ambitious corporate professionals get by on little sleep and instead take in ample doses of caffeine to feel awake. I used to be one of them as I used to drink up to 8 cups a day to keep myself going. When you drink coffee, the caffeine binds itself to a chemical in your brain called adenosine. Adenosine is a neurotransmitter in the brain that promotes sleep. When caffeine binds itself to adenosine, it stops adenosine from binding with the receptors in your brain and thereby stops you from feeling drowsy. As a result, you feel awake. However, drinking coffee is no substitute for sleep. In the short-term caffeine can help you regain your cognitive function after too little sleep, however, it does not cure the lasting and compounding effects of long-term sleep deprivation. Moreover, it makes you less emotionally stable, because caffeine causes your adrenal glands to flood your system with adrenaline, making you more emotionally-charged and possibly even irritable. So, mind your z's. Don't trade them for coffee. You need 7-8 hours sleep in order for your cognitive function to work optimally.

The fourth and last key fact I want you to know about your brain is that physical fitness is not just good for muscle tone, but also fundamental to supporting your cognitive function. How? First of all, exercise helps the brain by increasing the flow of blood, which delivers vital oxygen and glucose to the brain. This increases the delivery of energy to the brain. Secondly, aerobic exercise boosts the production of BDNF, which is short for Brain Derived Neurotropic Factor. BDNF is a protein that help turn brain stem cells into new neurons, which then helps the brain to develop new neural connections to repair failing brain cells, and to protect healthy brain cells, which in turn makes acquiring new knowledge and new memories easier.

So, as each of these four insights into how your brain operates has shown you, sacrificing your sleep, rest, exercise, and healthy eating at the altar of "working harder" directly undermines your brain power, which is key to you performance as a leader.

Today's leadership practice

Take a moment now to assess to what extent your current life choices are potentially hindering your physical ability to optimize your cognitive function. Reflect on each of the statements below and score your habits on a scale of 1 through to 5, 1 = never and 5 = always

- I always have breakfast [   ]
- I eat a meal or snack approximately every 3 hours throughout the day to maintain my energy levels [   ]
- I exercise on a regular basis, regardless of my circumstances. (meaning cardiovascular training at least three times a week and strength training at least once a week) [   ]
- I drink water throughout the day, eventually adding up to about half of my body weight in fluid oz [   ]
- I regularly get at least seven to eight hours of sleep [   ]
- I wake up feeling refreshed and energized [   ]
- I tend to choose foods that are both delicious and nutritious [   ]
- I take regular breaks during the day to truly renew and recharge [   ]

- I make time to eat lunch and I do NOT eat lunch at my desk [   ]

Take a moment now to review your answers and add up your scores. If you score is between 36 and 45 then you are already doing very well at managing your physical energy to support your cognitive function. If your score is below 36, then take some time now to reflect on why you are making the choices that are potentially hindering your physical ability to optimize your cognitive function. Don't judge, just reflect on them. How are you rationalizing those choices to yourself?

Financial savvy

Financial: adjective, relating to finance

Savvy: noun, shrewdness and practical knowledge; the ability to make good judgments.

C ash problems rather than profit issues cause 60% of business failures. Yet in business, most non-financial managers are focused on profit. They know that cash is king, but they wrongly believe cash management is the sole responsibility of the finance department and the CEO. However, the finance department is not responsible for how cash moves through the business. The daily decisions and actions of non-financial managers throughout the organization are what influences when cash is paid in and when cash is paid out. Non-financial managers are the ones who decide to extend credit to a customer to close a sale, which delays the cash inflow. Non-financial-managers decide how many product variations they want, which increases the amount of cash that is needed to maintain inventory etcetera. Each of these decisions impacts how cash moves through the company. The finance department just reports on it.

Moreover, effective cash management also improves profit, because it frees up cash to fund growth and reduces debt levels and thus increases revenues and lowers interest costs. So, cash management, also referred to as working capital management, is something any aspiring and existing leader should be interested in and focus on.

A financially-savvy leader should therefore not just aim to maximize profit, but also seek to minimize the amount of cash a company needs to operate, because that would maximize the company's free cash flow, which is the amount of cash a company could spend to drive growth and pay off debt after it has taken care of any capital investments to maintain a healthy business.

Today's leadership practice

1. Take a moment now to identify how strategic and operational decisions in your functional area are impacting your company's need for cash to operate.

2. Schedule a meeting with your business partner in the finance department to explore whether there are ways you and your team could do things differently to help reduce the need for working capital.

Trust destroying behaviors

Trust: noun, firm belief in the reliability, truth, ability, or strength of someone or something.

Destroying: present participle of the verb 'to destroy', put an end to the existence of (something) by damaging or attacking it

Behavior: noun, the way in which one acts or conducts oneself, especially toward others.

Trust is the foundation of leadership, because to follow a leader people must trust in the leader. Moreover, trust makes economic sense. Without trust, a leader needs to use approvals, punishments, micro management and an overblown hierarchical organization to make her people do the rights things, at the right time, in the right way. Such measures slow everything down and create negative side effects, including low engagement and high staff turnover, and thus add significant costs, making the organization both less productive and less profitable. However, despite the obvious importance of trust, research study upon research study has shown that trust in leadership is low. For example, Ernst & Young's "Global generations" study surveyed 9800 full-time employed professionals and found that less than half trusted those working above or alongside them. Why?

The reality is that most of us engage frequently and unwittingly in trust-destroying behaviors as we struggle with the pressures of meeting after meeting, difficult colleagues, pressing deadlines and stakeholders with different and often opposing expectations. For example, when did you last use flattery to convince someone to do something for you? Or put a spin on the facts to make it sound better or worse to support your point? Or overpromise and under deliver? Or snap at a colleague because you had a bad day? Or fail to share information to avoid being challenged on an issue? Or decide to quickly cover up a mistake? Or listen without seeking to understand? Or speak badly of someone in their absence? Or blame others for mistakes or bad results? Or fail to clarify expectations or hold yourself or others accountable? This is why building and maintaining trust is so hard as a leader. Every day, in everything you say or do or decide, you need to behave in ways that underscore your trustworthiness, that prove your genuine caring for the greater good, and that show your competence. To develop and maintain the necessary level of mindfulness, self-awareness and self-control to achieve this, will require daily reflection and practice.

Today's leadership practice

1. Review the list of trust-destroying behaviors below. Tick the box of any that you sometimes engage in.

    [ ] Sweet-talk someone
    [ ] Spin the truth
    [ ] Over-promise and under deliver
    [ ] Snap at a colleague
    [ ] Fail to share information
    [ ] Hide a mistake
    [ ] Listen without seeking to understand
    [ ] Gossip about someone
    [ ] Blame others
    [ ] Fail to clarify expectations
    [ ] Fail to hold yourself accountable
    [ ] Not deliver on your promise
    [ ] Play favorites
    [ ] Fail to praise someone who deserved it
    [ ] Other

2. For each of the behaviors which you selected, think of one recent example when you engaged in that behavior. Also note down what triggered you to behave like that.

3. For each of the selected trust-destroying behaviors, define what your "replacement

behavior" will be next time the same trigger occurs. This "replacement behavior" may just be a neutral placeholder behavior or a full-blown trust-building behavior.

Power

*noun, 1. the ability to do
something or act in a particular way,
especially as a faculty or quality 2. the
capacity or ability to direct or influence
the behavior of others or the course of
events.*

Power is not a very socially acceptable word. Many people associate it with being duplicitous, having sharp elbows, back stabbing, corruption, and manipulation, to name just a few. However, this interpretation overlooks the fact that one can have power and be a good and kind person. It all depends on how you choose to use your power, whether to help or to hinder others, and whether to serve yourself or the greater good. As a result of this negative attitude towards power, many people express an unwillingness to take action to attain power and to pursue power-based influence strategies. They instead believe that they can compete for the scarcity of positions higher-up in the organization purely on the merit of their good performance. Unfortunately, it usually doesn't work that way.

First, this approach assumes your superiors will be keenly aware of your performance. However, beyond your own boss, other superiors are rarely aware of your performance unless you have taken it upon yourself to do some effective self-promotion, which is something many people struggle with.

Secondly, this approach ignores the deciding role that personal, non-positional power (i.e. your network, expertise, and charisma) plays when those already in power have to choose between multiple people who are all performing equally well and have similar levels of expertise. For example, they might choose the person who has a much stronger relationship with the big bosses as a result of which the bosses already feel more familiar with them and thus more confident that he/she will be able to step up to the new role. Or they might choose the person who has developed a wider net of connections across the firm and is thus seen by the bosses to be better able to step into a bigger cross-functional role. Or they might choose the person who has built a reputation for workplace companionship (aka. colleagueship) across the business, making the bosses believe that it will be easier for them to be accepted as a new leader across the business

So, taken together, if you want to move into leadership then you need to both get noticed and develop your non-positional power to augment your results. Therefore, it is important to recognize that building and using power is an unavoidable part of becoming and being a leader. However, that does not mean you have to become cunning, devious and manipulative.

Today's leadership practice

There are three sources of personal (non-positional) power
- Skill and knowledge
- Persona/Charisma
- Connections

Take some time now to ponder the following questions to help you evaluate the strength of your own personal power against each of these dimensions:

1. Skill and knowledge: Are you a thought leader in your field or industry? Do people seek you out to get your opinion on an issue?

2. Persona/Charisma: Do your colleagues like you? Do they want to listen to you? Do they enjoy talking with you? Do they say nice things about you when you are not there?

3. Connections: Do you have a web of relevant reciprocal relationships, both internally and externally, that you can call on for assistance, support, advice, and information.

4. Lastly, ask yourself what, if any, actions could you commit to going forward to strengthen your personal power?

Self-determination

*noun, the act or power of making
up one's own mind about what
to think or do, without outside
influence or compulsion*

Self-determination creates a sense of ownership. When people are allowed to chart their own course, they feel a sense of control, they experience ownership, and they take pride in their work. However, many leaders often unwittingly destroy this sense of self-determination and ownership in their people. In their need for control, they unwittingly dis-empower and de-motivate their people by limiting their people's sense of self-determination. I on purpose say unwittingly, as this can happen even when you think you aren't micro-managing. For example, many leaders develop the vision for the team up in their ivory tower, only to share it with the team when it is done. But by doing so the team has no sense of ownership regarding the vision and the team will therefore not feel as engaged. Similarly, when a crisis occurs, a leader may go into "I will handle this" mode, playing the hero and protector. However, in doing so the leader just dis-engaged the team and also demotivated it by signaling that he or she does not believe the team could handle it.

So, creating an environment that allows employees to lead themselves, comes down to clarifying your beliefs and assumptions about what your people are capable of, how you value their input and how much oversight you believe they need. This requires careful soul searching and a mindful approach to your own actions as you lead every day.

Today's leadership practice

If you want to foster a self-directed culture in your team or department, then a good mantra to remember is that "less is more" in your leadership. So, take a moment now to reflect on your current situation. Are there any issues or areas where you could be less involved and rely more on your people's abilities to sort things out?

Leadership versus management

Leadership: noun, the action of leading a group of people or an organization

Management: noun, the process of dealing with or controlling things or people

For most of the 20th century the word leadership was used interchangeably with the word management to describe the act of directing workers. However, in the second half of the 20th century, when the western world transitioned to a knowledge-based economy, people started to differentiate between management and leadership, because if you want to have the full benefit of a knowledge worker's intellect and abilities, then telling him what to do won't work. Instead, you need to sell the knowledge worker on why he should do it.

Harvard professor John Kotter is one of the management thinkers who advocated for and clarified this differentiation, and his work has become the basis for how we nowadays differentiate between leadership and management. Kotter defined management as a set of well-known practices and procedures that make it possible to repeatedly produce products or services with a degree of order and consistency to key dimensions like quality and profitability. Management makes it possible to efficiently produce products and services within the context of the modern corporation. Management enables you to efficiently and effectively navigate the complexities of the many requirements, processes and people involved in producing products or services. Leadership, by contrast, he defined as a set of behaviors that would enlist people in a shared vision of the future, and that would inspire and motivate them to willingly commit their best efforts to realizing that shared vision. Leadership enables you to navigate the necessary change to generate the future and to generate growth.

So, based on Kotter's definitions we could summarize that management is about realizing our short-term goals. It is focused on the present and coordinates well-understood processes that lead to certain outcomes. Leadership on the other hand is future-focused. It deals with envisioning a possible better future, and it enlists, empowers and enables others to help make this a reality.

Today's leadership practice

1. Whether you head up a team, department, or a whole organization, the reality is that you need to practice both management and leadership. The tricky part is to get the balance right depending on what the team, department, or organization needs at that time, which is something that will keep changing depending on changing circumstances. So, take a moment now to evaluate how you balanced your time between leadership and management in the past week. Circle the 10 activities that took up all or most of your time in the past week. Then indicate whether that is a leadership activity by placing an "L" next to it, or a management activity by placing an "M" next to it.

   - Plan tactics [ ]
   - Communicate goals [ ]
   - Develop detailed plan to achieve results [ ]
   - Short-term planning [ ]
   - Develop future direction by assessing trends [ ]
   - Motivate and inspire [ ]
   - Set timetables [ ]
   - Seek commitments [ ]
   - Focus on improvement [ ]
   - Provide support [ ]
   - Align people [ ]
   - Allocate resource [ ]
   - Challenge the status quo [ ]
   - Control and problem solve [ ]
   - Focus on innovation [ ]

- Long-range planning [   ]
- Plan strategy [   ]
- Clarify the big picture [   ]

2. Based on the review of your activities in the past week, were you more focused on management or on leadership tasks? How does this fit with what your team/department/organization needs right now? What is your assessment of how well you are currently balancing management and leadership of your team/department/organization? Are you potentially over-managing and under-leading? Or are you under-managing and over-leading?

My own journey to leadership

From Ballerina to the C-Suite

As a child I was a real tomboy. I loved racing my bike (two white spots on my front teeth are lasting proof of what can happen when speed trumps skill) and building tree huts with my older brother. Then one day, when I was nine, I saw a documentary on TV with a call for auditions for the Royal Ballet School. I pleaded with my mom to let me have a go. I had started taking ballet classes only six months earlier. She saw no harm in letting me audition, so off I went. To everyone's surprise, I ended up being selected as one of 35 girls out of a group of 1,100 to join the School.

My mother was definitely not one of those dance moms. She had visions of me attending university, but not of me becoming a professional ballerina. Nevertheless, I spent the next six years training at the highest level. It was grueling, yet amazing. But while I loved dancing, and excelled at it, I aspired to a different life. After six years I dropped out to pursue an education, and ultimately, a professional career. I got a BA & MA in Economics and started my way up the corporate ladder, eventually becoming a Chief Marketing Officer.

I now run my company, SharpAlice, which provides online leadership development training for women, and recently one of my clients asked me what has most shaped me as a leader. I immediately thought of my mother. My father fell ill when I was seven, and she ended up single-handedly raising my two siblings and me. She always told us, "Where there is a will there is a way." She set a brilliant example that you can be both a kind woman and a badass. Then my client said, "Ok, but where did you get your ridiculous discipline, focus and search for continuous improvement?" And those traits, I realized, weren't instilled in me by my mother, but were actually the result of my ballet training. As a leader, I still draw on those and many other skills that I developed and honed during my time as a ballerina. So here is my recap of the five skills that took me from the ballet stage to the c-suite.

Never stop asking for feedback, because there's always room for improvement: At the Royal Ballet School, we had to bring a notebook with us to every class. After we finished, we had to write down any corrections we were given during the class. The next time we took that class, we were expected to have reviewed our list and focused on making those improvements.

That daily rhythm of feedback, improve, feedback, improve, established a mindset that has served me well throughout my career. Like everyone else, I was always encouraged when my bosses told me I did something well. However, I was always, and still am, more interested in hearing what I didn't do so well, and how I might improve.

Negative feedback is not something to fear. We can't assume that we'd do everything perfectly straightaway, so have the courage to ask for feedback, write it down if you need to, and improve it next time.

No-one else is going to lift that leg for you: I had a ballet teacher who used to shout this as we were doing our *développés,* a move whereby you extend your leg either high up to the front, to the side or to the back. It is a phrase that has stuck with me throughout my life as a mantra to remind me that if I truly want something, then I alone can achieve it.

Believe me, there have been plenty of times that I have thought, "Ugh, this is too hard!" But again, and again, this phrase has popped back into my mind as a reminder to just get on with it, as "no one else is going to lift that leg for you, Brenda."

You are capable of so much more than what you think. You just have to break it down and practice, practice, practice: Ballet is an incredibly unnatural discipline, physically speaking. My ballet teachers taught me how to break down these elaborate routines into achievable, sequential building blocks, eventually allowing me to conquer those complicated, unnatural yet beautiful poses and moves.

That is an experience and skill that has been fundamental to my career. It gave me the confidence that I could learn and teach myself any new skill I needed to succeed.

It also taught me that to learn those new skills, I had to just identify the key building blocks that made up each of those skills and then have the patience to gradually master them.

That confidence and approach, instilled in me by those years at ballet school, has helped me achieve new career milestones again and again. And even now, as I forge my way as a first-time entrepreneur, it is a critical part of my approach.

Always be aware of and in tune with your environment: Many people mis-categorize ballet as an individual endeavor. Indeed, ballet dancers must give their individual best, but at performance time, they have to actively collaborate with their fellow dancers, with the orchestra conductor and the musicians to bring the choreographer's vision to life. That means they have to be extremely aware of their environment at all times.

This art of reading and being in tune with your environment is a critical skill for any corporate leader. As a leader you are the choreographer of the vision and you guide your team to execute it. However, to be able to engage everyone to give their best to achieve that vision, you need to be incredibly attuned to the personal desires, challenges and needs of your team members.

Though my ballet training taught me this early on, it actually is a skill I often have to remind myself of, because as a leader who is often tasked with change management, and has a serious bias for action, I at times want to drive change too fast and literally have to whistle myself back and force myself to "dance to the beat."

The devil is in the detail: Ballet is all about precision and attention to detail, whether it's how you present a move or how you execute a choreography that takes you from one point on the stage to the next, or how you respond to the music.

When it comes to leadership, this attention to detail is often overlooked. People often think that attention to detail is for managers, who oversee the successful performance of specific tasks.

However, attention to detail is also critical for leadership. Not to micro manage, but to be able as a leader to pay attention to the critical details that make or break the success of a team or company.

Leadership requires one to both be able to see the big picture, but also to be able to see what the critical details are that will lead to the successful execution of that vision.

For me, this attention to detail, that was so core to my training as a ballerina, has therefore also been critical to my success as a leader. Without it I am just another leader with a big vision. With it, I am a leader with a vision and the ability to effectively deliver on it with my team.

Further reading & resources

Reading is an important source of learning and reflection for any aspiring and existing leader. I personally am a voracious leader and use any opportunity to read. I listen to a book on Audible whenever I walk our dogs or when I commute, and most nights when I'm too tired to do any further real work myself, I will pick up a book. When I read, I usually have a pen in my hand to highlight things and to take notes.

Below I've listed 11 books to help you deepen your reflections on how to strengthen and further develop your leadership.

1. Leading with questions: How leaders find the right solutions by knowing what to ask – by Michael J. Marquardt

2. Power: Why Some People Have It and Others Don't - by Jeffrey Pfeffer

3. Global Dexterity: How to Adapt Your Behavior Across Cultures without Losing Yourself in the Process - by Andy Molinsky
4. Leading with Questions: How Leaders Find the Right Solutions by Knowing What to Ask - by Michael J. Marquardt

5. The Obstacle Is the Way: The Timeless Art of Turning Trials into Triumph - by Ryan Holiday

6. Being Logical: A Guide to Good Thinking - by D.Q. McInerny

7. Leadership: In Turbulent Times - by Doris Kearns Goodwin

8. Humble Inquiry: The Gentle Art of Asking - by Edgar H. Schein

9. The Four Obsessions of an Extraordinary Executive: A Leadership Fable - by Patrick Lencioni

10. The Road to Character - by David Brooks

11. Questions Are the Answer: A Breakthrough Approach to Your Most Vexing Problems at Work and in Life – by Hal B. Gregersen

The Workshop

We offer a workshop to organizations to help their leaders to activate and implement the concepts presented in The Leadership Workout. The goal is to help leaders to become more intentional about their daily leadership through reflection and refinement of how they show up every day. For more information visit: https://theleadershipworkout.com/workshop/

Resources specifically for aspiring and existing female leaders

Explore SharpAlice.com, an online leadership development platform which enables women to take charge of their own leadership development by taking online courses to develop the skills to succeed as a leader. The courses (referred to as "leadership workouts") are tailor-made for women, addressing specific challenges women face on their leadership journey. Course topics range from how to improve your decision making, handle conflict, manage culture, build a high performing team and strengthen your leadership presence, to how to develop your financial literacy skills, improve your negotiating skills, build your influence, manage risk, communicate effectively, improve your emotional intelligence and much more.

Attend the SharpAlice Retreat, an exclusive 3-day opportunity for high-performing women to work with world-class experts and network with other trailblazing female leaders. For more information visit https://sharpalice.com/the-sharpalice-retreat/

About the author

Brenda van Camp-Elmes is the founder and CEO of SharpAlice, an online leadership development platform for women. Prior to founding SharpAlice, Brenda spend 20 years working as a marketing executive for consumer companies around the world. Most recently she was the Chief Marketing Officer of Blurb.com, the leading online publishing platform based in San Francisco. Prior to that, Brenda was the SVP, International Head of Marketing for the international fine art auction house Christie's. Earlier in her career, Brenda honed her business skills as a consultant for Booz Allen & Hamilton and Publicis Consultants and as an Investment Director for two European venture capital firms.

Having worked & lived in the US, Europe, Asia, and the Middle East, Brenda has a strong international orientation.

Brenda holds a BA and MA in Economics from the University of Amsterdam and professional coaching training from CTI's Co-Active Coach® Training Program, The Leadership Practices Inventory® (LPI) Coach program and the Presence-Based Coaching® program.

Brenda is originally from the Netherlands but nowadays she lives in Napa, California with her husband and two Labrador Retriever puppies, Dropje and Woody.

Brenda can be contacted at:
brenda@theleadershipworkout.com

Also visit:
Theleadershipworkout.com
SharpAlice.com

Index